POETIC RECIPES

FOR

HUNGRY HEARTS

Poetic Recipes for Hungry Hearts

Written by Tracy Shefras
Printed and Published by KDP Amazon 2023
First Published 2022

Front Cover design by Tracy Shefras with Canva.com
Interior images Canva.com

To Helen
From One Author
to
Another

For Light Reading

Much
Love
Trauyxe

CONTENTS

A man's work is nothing but this slow
trek to rediscover, through the detours of art,
those two or three great and simple images
in whose presence his heart first opened.

Albert Camus

And A Woman's!

Appetiser

Hello Dear Reader

Many of the following verses arrived
in my head and I seized a pen
having heard the first line and wrote
it down. This might
happen on a walk, in the middle of
the night or whilst driving - bit
inconvenient really! I either
rushed home to capture it, or
logged the sentiment or first
sentence into my head. Then, on
reaching home, I wrote it out by
tuning back into those sentiments.
Often I completely forget what I
heard or thought. At first this was a
bit frustrating but then I learnt
to let go and trust that if it was
important enough it would return.

Often it does and often in disguise,
such is life.

At times I felt the urge to write a poem as a knowing. Life clicked into place and it seemed apt and fitting to write it as a marker for myself. This is reflected in Medicinal Rhyme No Reason on page 1.

It has been an act of listening. Tuning my ear to my own particular muse, which if you read Birdsong on page 6, you will see that process having taken metaphorical shape.

This process has taught me many things about life. About the human cycle not only through our 24 hour clock but also in connection with the larger cycle of life, The Universe and how we all fit together, often snuggly and on occasion not so comfy.

Slowing down and appreciating what is right under the nose seems to be key. Most of these poems have acted as lassoes to bring my attention present and act in accordance with my best interest at heart.

The poems have revealed their own personality - a surprise to me. They seem to act as aunts, uncles, family members, or close friends, guiding me and keeping me on my yet unknown destination. All I can do is put one foot after the other and watch the unfolding. Bit like a parent that is child-led in the rearing of children - I am poetry-led.

I hope, Dear Reader, that you enjoy my culinary delights, in word form, and perhaps like myself, receive some kind of

nourishment from them, or
simply just enjoy the act of
reading.

Perhaps, too, you might be
inspired to start your own
musings, (if you haven't already)
however they appear, like
Birdsong suggests. I have left
some pages blank at the back
should that happen.

Happy Reading
Tracy

ps. I have made audio versions of
quite a few of them. If you would
like to hear some of them please
get in touch at...

recipeshungryhearts@gmail.com

I Make my own Medicine
Two Drops of Words
A Few Lines
Some Trendy Adjectives
The Occasional Pun
A Drop of Fun
A Verse or Twenty
To Share I have Plenty
Come to my Apothecary
We'll Write you a Prescription
From a Place Unknown
Delivering Medicine
You'll No Longer Moan
For our Brews are Many
Few and Far In-between
But Ultimately
All the Same
To make the Soul Clean
The Spirit Soar
The Body Agile
The Mind Clear
With a Holistic Outlook
Holding All Life Dear

Medicinal Rhyme No Reason
Extract from 'Knowing'
23rd July 2018

Everything points to Love
Back to Self-Care
To Opening The Heart
Everything
Doubt Not!
Love is the Answer

Lay your fingers gently
On the Hedgerow and
Feel
Love Returning
Be Patient
It may take a while
But with Daily Repetition
It happens Quicker
And Quicker

Get Thee to The Hedgerow
Touch
Touch The Hawthorn
The Nettles
The Ferns
And the Docks

Caress them like you may
Touch the hand of a new born
baby
Just as gently as almost not
Touching At All

Caress Them and Feel Their
Caress
Come right back at
You
Seeping into your body
Returning you to Truth
To Love

Touch the Hedgerow
It's got Magical Potent Properties
You will know who you are
With the Hedgerow

The Hedgerow has lined
A Thousand Lanes
A Million Highways
Umpteen Paths
To Walk Upon
She has seen It All
She knows you better
Than You Know Yourself

She has seen you Pass By
Generation after Generation
Decade after Decade
Into Centuries
Through Millenia
She is as Ancient
As they Get

Touch Her and See
What she has to Offer
Become One with Her
Hedge Your Bets
And lay your whole Hand
Right Down On Her
Now

There is
No Bluffing
No Hiding
No Pretence

When you let Yourself
Meet the Hedgerow
It's Just Obvious What Matters

HRT for The Heart
(Hedgerow Restoration Therapy)
Poem from The In-Between
20th August 2019

When my Core
Speaks to Your
Core
We Core Relate
Like Two Apples
On a Tree
Side by Side
Happy growing Together
Taking up as Much
Space as they Need
And if Not
Nudging one another
A little
To allow the other
To expand
or Contract
As needs BE
That's the Core Relationship
It's Give and Take
In Equal Measure
Not always at
The Same Time
But Mostly
Just Hanging Out
Balanced

Core
17th June 2022

Listen to Me
Listen out for Me
If you can
Tune your Ear
To My Song
If not Imagine my
Glorious Tweet
Just a Whisper
Away
I am portable
Listen for me, or
Start your own
Birdsong
and you will feel
Comfort and Ease
Lightness and Happiness
Enter your Being
I am Portable
Tune your Ear
To My Song
And let me
Soothe Your
Weary Soul
Or Inspire your
Creative Muse
I am Portable
I want you to hear me
Why else do I sing
But to grab your attention
And draw it to what matters most
I am Portable
Hear Hear

Birdsong
Extract from 'An Extended Whisper'
20th March 2022

I have Ridden
The Vine Before
But I didn't know It
I was just coasting through life
With immortality sharp on my
Heels
Invincibility by my Side
and Passion Tugging
Begging Me to Keep Up
And I did

I didn't know it
But I felt it
There is a Difference
Between Knowing and Feeling
Once you know what you
Are feeling then you can begin
To master and direct
That which is Sustaining you
Or perhaps depriving you
Or even making you thrive
You can join in
Simply
Simply
Simply
Join In

With your Own Thread
Your Own Vine
Of this Tightly Knitted
Holy Planet Pattern
And Assume the shape
You want to be
Are BornTo Be
Regardless of the shapes appearing around
You
You can Determine the
Bigger Picture
Oh what joy

Knit One Pearl Won
Extract from 'Riding The Vine'
3rd December 2021

We are in the Middle of
An Energetic War
Call it Yin Yang
Masculine Feminine
Left Right
Nature Versus Humans
X Chromosome
Why
Call it what you Want
Him V Her
Them and Us
Patriarchy V Matriarchy
But why not just Call it
What it IS
UNCOMFORTABLE
Frightening
Scary
Unsafe
Traumatic
Crisis
Tipping Point
SAY IT AS IT IS
Don't Pussyfoot
That's what made it
PUSSYFOOTING AROUND
Call it what it is
Unsafe
Unstable
Unreliable
Predictably
Unpredictable
On a Knife Edge

And when you are done with Labels
Step BACK and Assess
What is it you can do
To Alleviate
Shift
Invite some kind of Balance
What is it You Can Do
To Restore Safety
Start Right Under Your Nose
Right on Your Own Doorstep
Make Yourself Safe
SO SO Safe
That there is not one thing
That can knock you off Kilt
Make Safety Security
And Balance Your Intention
Get Yourself Safe
On Safe Ground
And then you can be of some
Use
Without Safety As the
Foundation of a
Strong Life
Everything will
Keep Toppling
Get Safe
Crack Your Own Code

EggShells
Poems from 'The In-Between'
1st October 2019

Hop up Here
Way up High
Onto myEagle's Perch
And see what I see
Look down from here
At everything
And take stock
View the world from
My Macro Vision
If you can
And get perspective
I am Portable
Hop up, take a leap of faith
And soon you will
See you way through
Your troubles
Whatever they
Are
Hop up if you can
Or if not
Do it in your Mind's eye
I am Portable
Up here all is what is
What is
Not what it seems
Take a Peak

Eagle's Perch
Extract from 'An Extended Whisper'
24 March 2022

Stay in your frequency
Do everything possible to be
In That
That who You Are
Connect from that place
and keep returning
so as not to forget
It's where you Strength lies
in your Frequency
You can experience other
Frequencies
But make sure you have
a Strong Bond with Your Own
like a mother and toddler
inseparable
in those early years
Stay attached to your
Frequency
Be sure of who you
Are
And then you can go
And do anything
Regardless
For you know you have
A home
To return to
Your Frequency
Treasure it

The Holy Grail
Extract from 'Caught in The Nick of Time'
12 June 2022

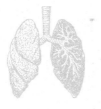

Apply Breath
A Topical Balm
Smear it
All Over
Lovingly
Thoughtfully
Intimately
And as you Smooth
and touch upon
Such a Medicinal Moment
Stay Awhile
In the application
As if to Log the
Therapy
Right Down Into
The deepest place
That you may or may not
Know yet
Log it in
As an intention
A smooth clean fresh Breath
Full of Possibility
Full of Promise
Full of Potential
Apply the Balm
Your Breath
topically
but internally too
like you would to a wounded
Knee
a grazed elbow
an open cut
with such care

and attention
that it knows it is seen
felt
heard
the breath will then know
it has come into
your orbit as
something of a
Priority
Apply the balm
topically
everyday
until finally
The Breath knows how to
Behave
In your Best Interest
Moving You
Only to Heart Centred
Action

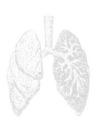

Inhaling and Exhaling
Extract from 'A Quantum Leap'
19th January 2022

In the In-Between Again
Just do Stuff
Anything
Just do it
Try not to be too
Clever
Or Inventive
Or Dynamic
Bide Time
Until
Until That Moment
And then you will know
How to Act
Bide Time
Know the Rising is Coming
It has to come
Cause the Gates of Grief
Opened
You don't know when
Or for how long
You just know
The energy will Rise
And you will find
Yourself doing
The Impossible
Unheard of
Unimaginable
You just will
And you will Ask Yourself
Why Now
Why not last Week
Last Year
Why Now

And this time
You Will Know Why
Just Because
Just Because you can
Divine Timing is Ticking Through you
Your Rhythm and Clock has
Synced with Nature
You will stay in Tune
Until when you don't know
All you know
Is that now you are one Step
Closer
To knowing the Process
Understanding your own Workings
Knowing what to do
One step closer is Good Enough for you
You'll take it
High Five
Cheers
Thanks A Billion Trees

Divine Timing
Extract from 'The In-Between'
Easter Sunday 21st April 2019

Stare at Me
If you can
Or call me to mind
See me in Your Minds' Eye
I am portable
Watch me wax and wane
And if you dare
catch me when I'm full
And keep staring
And as you do
You will begin to feel everything
In you
Soften
Relax
Yield
Turn to joy
Turn to love
Turn to Presence
Stare at me
Through my monthly
Cycle as I wax and wane
Everyday
If you can
Or call me to mind
If not catch me when
I'm full
I am portable
I want to share my gifts
I am a full moon

A Full Moon
Extract from 'An Extended Whisper'
19th March 2022

I could turn back
I have done many times
But not on Purpose
I just haven't been able to
Proceed
And now, today, this time
I am in the same place
But in a Different Awareness
Mindset
I have a Choice
Proceed
Or Turn Back
Perhaps even Be Turned Back
But today is different
I have seen the Light
Just a Flicker of It
It's Strong and Guiding Me
Forever
I will Proceed
I have to Proceed
I am Bored of Turning Back
The Horizon looks Inviting
Even though I cant see it Yet

A Rendezvous with Clarity
Extract from 'On the Brink of Abundance'
18th January 2022

We are Vessels
Vessels of Change
We Float
Just because We Can
We have learnt how
To Float
Regardless of
The Weather
We hope others
Will Learn To Float
Too
It's such Fun
Bobbing and
Gulping
And sometimes
Sinking
Then Resurfacing
It's almost an
Addiction
A healthy Addiction
To find the
Surface
And Rise
And Roar
At the New Dawn
The New Day
And
Know
That everything
That happened
Yesterday is no
longer Valid
We can do this

We Can Float
In all kinds of
Water
Murky
Sludgy

Swirly
Rubbly
Cresting
Sinking
We love it all
The Water has our
Backs

We can Float
We can Float
We can Float

Dive in
It's Divine in
Here
Glorious
Unimaginable
Don't worry about
What to bring
Just bring it all
And Trust
That the Water
Has Got your
Back

You can just
Float
And you will
Be Carried to
Exactly where you
Need to Be

In the Here and
Now
In Beauty
In Nature
In your Deepest
Soul Truth
It's All just
Waiting for you
To Choose the
Moment that you dive
In and join with all
The Others
Floating and
Receiving From
The Divine Edge of Life
Have A Whale of A Time

Rewild Yourself.....If Not Now, When
Poem from The Edge of Water
3rd June 2020

And that Day Came
And She…..He/It/They/Them
Just sank into The Energy
All striving for Knowledge
subsided
All of Them
Just Let Go
Of Needing To Know
And Trusted
that what would Rise, would
Rise
The Relentless Spirit
Could carry on
doing it's thing
It was never going to
Stop
But in the Meantime
She Choose to be Still
And know that She Is That

BioFeedback from So Hum
Extract From 'Completely Waxed'
16th April 2022

And suddenly
All those things you did
You no longer do
Something has replaced them
All that time you
Wasted
Is now invested
In something far more
Profitable
Not in the
Financial sense
But that may come
But more as
Investment of
Good self care
Which in turn breeds
More of the same
You have hoicked
By some mad luck
You mind out of the underworld
For long enough to
Give it purpose
And mission
And a new you
How the fuck did
You do that
People die down there
Kill themselves
People never manage
To stay up long enough to allow
New habits
Healthy behaviours
Ways
To form
How did you do that
Here's how

You decided not to believe anything
you decided
To just be present
Let your emotion
Flow
You didn't block your natural
Energies
You unclogged your system
Your
Constipated energetic system
Had a right royal flush
And
You would like to say that it was
Just one pull of the flush
But it wasn't
Perhaps it could have been in
different Circumstances
But it was just you
Only you to rely on
And that's the long and the short of it
We all only have just us
We have to flush
Ourselves through
Of the past
Everything
We have to build a momentum
Inside ourselves
That returns us
To full function
Full cleanse

We have to do it for ourselves
We can ask for help
But mostly it's our
Business

We have to flush the Debris
Of generation after generation
of Crazy Energy
Right through our systems
Colonic irrigation if you like
Spiritual - even

High IQ - Bog Standard Living
Poem to Coax Us Up Through The Quagmire
29th November 2019

You'd think by Now
You'd recognise the Signs
But you Don't
They keep Fooling You
They turn up
Disguised
Yet so Obvious
And each Time
You fall for Being Fooled
And you Laugh
At your Own
Inability to Recognise
The Nature of Your Own
Mischievous Soul
Playing with You
To see if you are up to the Job Yet
To deliver the Goods
Say it as it is
And Finally
Get the Punchline of your Own Life
WAKE UP
PAY ATTENTION
Split Your Sides Laughing

Soul Ace - The Cosmic Joker
Poem from The In-Between
9th May 2020

My energy is flowing
And I just realised it
How come I'm the last to know

It's got no stops no blocks big enough
To shunt my growth
I am free
How come I'm the last to know

I just felt it
Pulsing through me
Oh so familiar yet so unknown
Forgotten
But now I remember
How come I'm the last to know

My energy is flowing
That's my new story
It's a simple tale
With ebb and flow
How come I'm the last to know

My energy is flowing
Even when I'm quiet
Even when I'm small
Even when I'm hiding
It's still flowing
How come I'm the last to know

My energy is flowing
Even when I rest
It has a subtle accepting quality that
says
Just let go

My energy is soaring
I can feel it come from the
depth Of the Planet
Of the Cosmos
Of Me
An unknown untraumatised
Place
It's got an unknown quality
To it
I'm the first to know

Liminal
June 2018

I can't see me
Where am I
Smothered in you
What am I to do
I keep chopping and
changing
Why is that so
No sense of myself
Not even my Ego

Oh where did I go
Oh where did I go
Oh where did I go

Where did I go this time
I have no idea
Hijacked and hooked
Away
Before I even could say
Hey
NO
NOT TODAY
I have stuff to do
And if I'm not here
I cant get it done
Where did I go this time

I've had it up to here
Where did I go
When will it stop
Departing brings woe

Oh where did I go
Where did I go this Time

I feel the tears
It's ME returning
I have a choice now
Turn away
Or let Loves Burn In

Oh where did I go

Oh there I am
I am yielding and
Feeling and letting
It in
Oh there I am
Please Lord stop with
This Sin

I want to stay
To stay forever
I can't stand the pain
Of hell bent for leather

So I beg you now
Who ever you are
Please just STOP
I have had enough
I want to LIVE
Not disappear in a
PUFFFFF

Re Emergence E
Extract from 'Rest Q Remedies'
29th July 2018

Keep your Wound
Close By
don't abandon it now
this is the most
important relationship
of your life
your wound
it is the source
the font
the well of all
your power
keep it close by
closer than the next breath
consult it on every action
check regularly
keep it close by
your wound
now you have found it
don't let it go again
don't abandon it again
keep it close
by
like a new born child
right in the centre of your
heart it has much to offer you
keep it close by

Please

Forget-Me-Not
Extract from "The Light of Day"
Timeless

I Listen to Thee
Oh Tree
As though we are
Separate
Telling me what to do
What to write
Please Tell Me What
To Wear
Sometimes I
Despair
Oh what a Privilege
To be Mothered by
Thee

Imagine how busy I'll Be
If I listen to
The Whole of Nature
And not just Thee
Oh Tree
Oh Tree

Perhaps I Already Am
So Naive a Human
Can Be
Surely you will Send
Me Support
Reinforcements
A new Quill
By Which to Take
Dictation
A Secretary Even

How Fooled I am
By My Own
Glow

The Whispers I hear
Are but my own Mind
My Own Truth
Turned back on Me
In the Presence of
Thee
Oh Tree
Oh Tree

I'd rather attribute
The Brilliance to
Someone Else
Something Else
Other Than accept
And Humble May It Be
That Maybe
Just Maybe
I am at One
With
Such
Poetic Justice

Night Whispers of an Urgent Type
Poem From The In-Between
25th April 2019 - 3 in The Morning

Unpack
Your
Brain
Feed
Your
Mind

Brain Coral
Extract from 'Use It Or Lose It'
31st July 2022

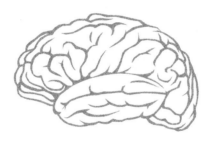

Flying flying flying
And suddenly you are flying
And its easy
It's new
And all your bird family are
Flying along side you
And you feel your
Wings so Strong
And flapping flapping
Through the sky
Blue sky
Rainbows
Horizons
Treetops
Crescent Moon
Stars
Lakes
And you need to
Flap your wings again
To get the consistency
Ah, this feels so nice
So different
Yet familiar
You are higher
Than you ever thought
Possible
And you are gliding
Soaring
Over Mountains
Glaciers
Snow Topped Peaks
This is beyond
Photography

You are a living
Expression of a well
Developed Colour
Picture
Oh What a Picture
And you just know
You were built for this
This is you
There is no other way
To exist
Flying and flapping
And
Collapse
....
....
....
....
Start all over again

Sacred Geometry for Fledglings
14 September 2018

Look up at Us
If you can
Or see us in your Mind's Eye
We hang out in the Sky
All sorts of white fluffy delights
We hold much Rain
Tell us where to travel to
To which parts of the world
Where water is needed
To drink
To put out fires
To pour down upon thirsty
land
Look up at Us
Help us Hear
The Parched Call
We want to be effective
Look up at Us
If you can
Or call us to Mind
We are Portable
Send us to where
Your Prayers go
To quench this thirst
We are Portable
Willing and able

Clouds
Extract from 'An Extended Whisper'
25th March 2022

I place Pit Stops
on my Vine
To Catch Relentless
Spirit
As it Knows
No Bounds
Like a Mother
With a Toddler
I set Up A Routine
To ensure
Resting
Food
Water
Social Interaction
And Primarily
Reconnection
With Source
The Manager
Source
The Inspirer
Source
The Driving Force
The Root of The Vine

I set it all Up
In Order
To Stay Sane
Or Else I might be Joining
The likes of Van Gogh

An Artistic Paradox
Still On the Brink of Something
4th January 2022

I am moved, I am
But only if you are
Please be moved
Then I can be moved
Too
Co-dependent I am
I want to laugh
But you must laugh first
Please laugh
I want to laugh
Co-dependent I am
Go on, shed a tear
I want to cry too
Please cry, I want to
Cry too
Co-dependent I am
I need you to have Faith
Then I can have Faith
I beg you, please have
Faith
Co-dependent I am, Thats me!
Allow yourself, go on
Let yourself go
I want you to let yourself go
Please let go
Then I can
Remember I'm Co-dependent
I see your resistance
No doubt about that
Co-dependent I am
Please don't resist
Ok, I'll try

I'll try and go first
It's not going to be easy
Co-dependent I am
Look I'm laughing
You can laugh too
Go on, chuckle a bit
Here let me help
Now I can shed a tear
All by myself
Join in if you want
If you need
Discover Communion
Not wealth
I can feel happiness
Creeping up in me
Let's share it together
There's no harm in some Glee
Look we did it
We moved we cried
We laughed together
There's no need for
Permission
Emotion not meant for the
Tether
Thanks for joining in
Collaborating, sharing
Let's try free expression Loving
and
Caring

Ubuntu
17th December 2017

I have no Edges
There is nothing to Hold
Onto
I am free falling
It's scary at first
But then
I reckon
I will land
On a big white
Fluffy cloud
Like Cotton wool
Cushioned
Cushioned
Cushioned
Surely this is belonging

Certainty No Longer
Looks
Appealing
Uncertainty seems
A no brainer
So much possibility
I am ready to cut
My own umbilical cord
and float free
whilst still in my
body
With light
and Grace
And a smile Too

The darkness is ready
To deliver it's goods
It is primed
Marinated enough
The hermetically sealed
Process is almost done
The cauldron that I am
is now ready to project
beauty
love
grace
hope
spirit
trust

Boundaries are an illusion
Were an illusion
I used to be ignorant of them
but now I see their use
like a holding
a family
a collective hug
until the light wants to burst
Through
Can burst through
and violate every
belief system ever held
Into presence
Just presence
a trance worthy of
Global Entitlement

No Edges
An Extract from 'Unbounded'
5th March 2022

Put Your Feet
In The Earth
On The Earth
Naked
Not You
Your Feet
Naked
But You as Well
If You Fancy
Put Your Feet
On Our Mother
Our Earth
Connect
Do it Everyday
For as long as You Can
As often as Possible
Soul to Sole
Sole to Soil
Put Your Feet
On Earth
And Imagine What's Possible
Just Stand there
Or Walk Around
On Earth
And Allow
Allow Earth to Seep
Into Your Being
Into Your Core
Allow Her to
Show You What To Do
Allow Earth's Instruction Manual
To Download into

Your Being
And You be Guided to Follow
Instructions
Earth's Instructions
Allow Earth to Speak
Directly
To You
In the Perfect Language
You Understand
And then You Shall have no Doubt
For it is as If You Speak to
Yourself
Get Earthed
Get Ego Neutralised
Get Grounded
Get Seeded with the One that
Knows Best
Sprout from Connection
Rise
And Feel what it is like
To be Permanently Attached
Linked In
Plugged Into
The Only Life Support System You
Will Ever Need

Remember?
Extract from Poem from The In-Between
22nd June 2019

Visit Me
If you Can
And
Stay awhile
if not, make it
brief then carry me
in Your Mind's Eye
and as you do
having touched me lightly
It's likely you will
feel a
stirring
as your heart
begins to open
Carry me in your
Mind's Eye
I am Portable
tune in
think of me
wherever you are and then
One Day
you will perhaps think
you have dropped me
but No
on the contrary
now I am
inside you
forever
we have united
and
collaboration can
happen in
the blink of an eye
I am portable

Yew
An Extended Whisper
12th January 2022

In Your Frequency
You will Know
Exactly What to Do
Doubt Not
Not even a Thought
For This and That
You will Just
Flow
Be Natural
and
Be at Complete
Peace
In all Your Actions

In Your Frequency
Life Just Happens
Moment to Moment
Everything is Taken
Care of

Your Frequency will
Guide You
Naturally
Effortlessly
Easily
Into Each
Moment
All you have to do
Is Say
YES

And
If you find Yourself
Vacating
Abandoning
Neglecting
Rejecting

Even ditching Your Frequency
In favour of an apparent what might
seem like
Something Better
If you desert Your Frequency
Your frequency
Will rapidly
Call You Home
Like gently grabbing
A Toddler
About to run into the Road
Your Frequency
Will guide you Back to
Yourself
Back to Your Frequency

You will never have to
Worry again
Fret
Panic
Get anxious
Your Frequency will
Take care of it All

All you have to
Do
Is make Space
For Your Frequency
To Emanate Through You
Pulse Through You

Flow Through You
Be You
How lucky Are You
You and Your Frequency
In Magnetic Cahoots
FanFrequencyTastic

Seeing The Wood For The Trees
Extract from 'Bespoke Poems'
19th June 2022

Lannding the Mind
Not too far forward
Nor way behind
Guide it into
Its Docking Station
Steady
Slowly
Seemlessly
then
Let it Stabilise
Get used to its
New Resting Place
Find comfort and Ease

Prodigal Hope
An Extract from 'The Relentless Spirit'
11th February 2022

From Nowhere
The impulse arrived
To strengthen an already
Well lived and comfortable life
I was destined to care for more
An unplanned calling
But embraced entirely

All the best things in me
Suddenly magnified
For I was Tethered to Truth
And by some strange magic
I managed to keep the vision
Of a better future
Safe for many years

And then I dropped
The guardianship ball
For I did not know
That I was growing
On such rocky ground
But somehow I managed

Just recently
I felt the same impulse
Again
And now the seed of
What's Next
Gestates inside
But no child in sight

Just the potential
Of my own Big Bang
Into creation
Oh God
I hope this time
I stay tethered to truth

Tethered To Truth
Extract From 'Bespoke Poems"
February 2021

OMG I'm Living the
Dream
But the Nightmare
Still lies in bed with me
I roll over and comfort it
It's ok, I say
You are a Nightmare
You will aways be a Nightmare
But let's support the Dream
Together
The Nightmare lies still and
Ponders
I reach out my hand to it
Lay it gently on its head
It's ok I say
We can breath Together
As One
It flinches a little
In disbelief
Please just trust me I say
Lets give the Dream a chance
We both let out this huge
Exhale
That sweeps all the dust into the air
It's such a big exhale it goes on forever
I lie
Infact it's a lot of all types of breaths
Holding Panting Long Drawn out
Breathing
Huge great big gulps more panting
Never Ending

I get a bit woozy
The Nightmare seems to
Mirror me
We move closer and cling on tight
As we breath and pant and gulp and
Give Breath to the New US
We have to be born
Together
We are two sides of the same coin
Twins
Soul Mates
Dark and Light
We exist as One Together and
Separate
The dust particles spiral up
In the air
Mixing and melting and merging
With each other in
Blind Collusion
Full of delicious and bright
Shiny Sparkly Space Dust
The Darkness sits bolt
Upright
OOOOh this feels good
How come I didn't know about it
I've got to go tell the
Rest of the Darkness
They are going to Love this
I take Its hand and say
NOT YET
Rest a while
Let's just savour the
Moment
For the both of Us
This is Ours
Let's get used to it
So we don't
Slip back too far
And forget
This Beautiful Place

It looks at me
Ok I'll trust you on this
It lies back down
And snuggles into Me
Our breath seems to have
Synchronised
OMG I think
We Are Living The
Dream
The Darkness leans over and says
Hey
Remember
Rest a while
This is for
US
Rest
I smile
I snuggle in closer and
Our Breath is no longer separate
I can hardly tell where It begins
And I Start
It is as if our bodies merged into one
With no lines of
Distinction
I feel the Darkness
Put Its hand on my head
And soothe me
Rest It says
Here
Drink Your Own Medicine

The Darkness Speaks Back
Day One - Under The Holly Tree
28th June 2018

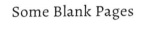

Some Blank Pages

For

Your Own Musings

Printed in Great Britain
by Amazon